Everything You Need to Know About

AN ALCOHOLIC PARENT

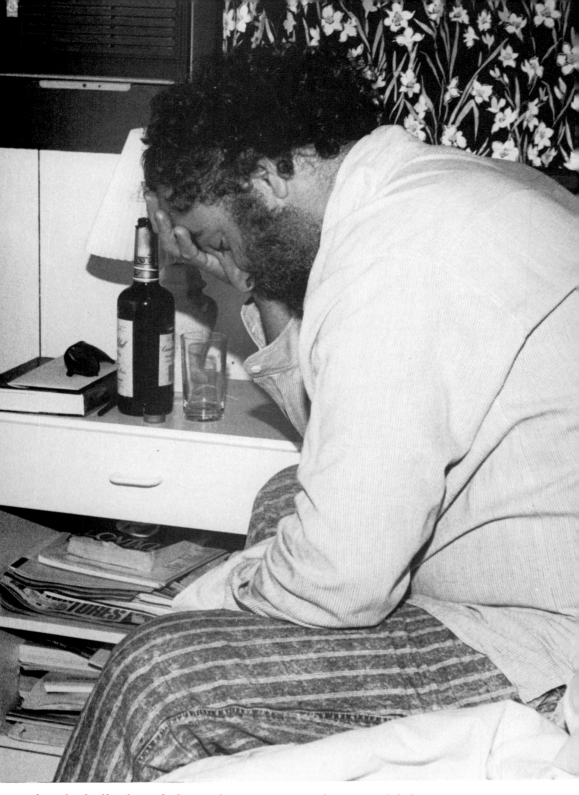

An alcoholic doesn't know how to stop at just one drink.

Everything You Need to Know About

AN
ALCOHOLIC
PARENT

Nancy Shuker

Series Editor: Evan Stark, Ph.D.

THE ROSEN PUBLISHING GROUP, INC.
NEW YORK

Published in 1990, 1993, 1995 by The Rosen Publishing Group, Inc.
29 East 21st Street, New York, New York 10010

Revised Edition 1995

Copyright © 1990, 1993, 1995 by The Rosen Publishing Group, Inc.

Manufactured in the United States of America.

Library of Congress Cataloging-in-Publication Data

Shuker, Nancy.
   Everything you need to know about an alcoholic parent.
   (The Need to know library)
   Includes bibliographical references and index.
   Summary: Offers advice on how to deal with an alcoholic and where to go for help.
      ISBN 0-8239-2114-X
      1. Alcoholism—Juvenile literature. 2.Children of Alcoholics—Juvenile literature. [1. Alcoholism. 2. Alcoholics.]
      I. Title. II. Series.
      HV5066.S49 1989
      362.29'23—

                             89-10703
                                CIP
                                AC

Contents

Introduction

An alcoholic is someone who is addicted to alcohol. This means that when an alcoholic starts drinking, he or she cannot stop. Alcoholics have a disease called alcoholism. They depend on alcohol to relax, have fun, or even talk with their family. The alcoholic loses control when he or she drinks. There are many kinds of alcoholic drinks including beer, wine, wine coolers, and whiskey. All are equally dangerous if abused.

Having an alcoholic parent is very difficult. Your parent's disease affects the whole family. It may make you feel embarrassed and alone. It's important to remember however, that you are certainly not the only one who has an alcoholic parent. Many other kids may have the same kind of homelife as you. It may surprise you to know that in your class at school, probably four or five of your classmates are living with an alcoholic parent.

There is much to learn about alcoholism. Knowing about the disease may help you to be happier at home, and be more successful at the things that you like to do. This book will tell you how to be independent from your parent with an alcohol problem. You will learn that you don't have to feel guilty or responsible for your parent's sickness. It has nothing to do with you.

You can also learn how alcohol changes your family's relationships with each other. Once you understand this, you will be better able to lead your own life. This book can help you start to be your own person. On your own, or with professional help, you can separate yourself from your parent's alcoholism. You can make choices that are right for you. You can still care about your alcoholic parent, but you deserve to find your own happiness.

Many people enjoy one or two alcoholic drinks with their meals.

Chapter 1

Alcoholism: a Definition

People used to think alcoholism was a moral flaw. Only weak people could become alcoholics. Alcoholics just didn't have any self-control. If they were good people they would just stop drinking.

Today, we know that alcoholism is not a moral weakness. It is a disease. No one chooses to be an alcoholic, and asking an alcoholic not to drink is like asking someone in a wheelchair to walk. They would if they could.

Many adults drink alcohol on occasion. They drink when they get home from work, to relax. They drink when they have dinner. They drink to celebrate. They may even get drunk once in a while. That does not mean that they are alcoholics.

Most likely, these people are social drinkers.
They can choose to drink, or just as easily not to
drink. They hardly ever drink too much, and
their bodies tell them when they've had too
much.

The Start of Alcoholism

Alcoholics usually start out as social drinkers.
But for some reason, they begin to drink more
and more. Often they can drink more than other
people and feel fewer effects. This is called
developing *tolerance.*

With time, they become dependent on
alcohol. An alcoholic cannot function without a
drink. His or her brain cells change after a while;
whereas in the beginning he or she had to
struggle to cope under the effects of alcohol, now
he or she has problems dealing with being sober.

Only 3 to 5 percent of alcoholics are skid row
bums. Most have normal jobs, normal families,
normal-looking lives. They don't stand out so
much because drinking is so common. However,
they need help just as desperately as any
homeless alcoholic.

The Disease's Effects

Alcoholism progresses in four stages. The first of
these, the warning stage, is when someone just
begins to feel the addiction. The alcoholic begins
to look for reasons to get drunk more often, and

will make anything an excuse to have a drink. His tolerance rises as his body becomes used to having alcohol in it. He goes from an occasional drink to drinking daily.

In the next stage, the danger stage, the alcoholic becomes drunk more often. He may begin to experience *blackouts*, periods of time he does not remember. He drinks alone, sneaks drinks, gulps drinks, feels guilty about his drinking but doesn't stop. He begins to miss work because of his drinking.

In the third stage, or the losing-control stage, the alcoholic starts to blame others for his problem. He withdraws and becomes unpredictable. He loses all sense of responsibility. He withdraws from family and friends, and sometimes has to be hospitalized because of alcohol.

The final stage is the loss-of-control stage. The alcoholic will accept any kind of drug, not just alcohol. He no longer makes excuses for his behavior, and his only comfort comes from a bottle. He shakes if he doesn't have a drink every few minutes. He can't do anything right. Often, the alcoholic develops all kinds of other diseases that are side effects of alcohol abuse, such as cirrhosis of the liver, high blood pressure, heart damage, and brain damage.

There is no fifth stage, because if the progress of alcoholism is not stopped, it always results in insanity or death.

Why My Parent?

No one knows why some people become alcoholics and some don't. There are many theories about this. One theory says that there are some people who have low levels of *endorphin* in their bodies. Endorphin is a chemical that makes the body feel numb naturally, and calms you down. If you have too little endorphin in your system, you might seek out alcohol as a replacement. Alcohol also suppresses endorphin production in the body over time, which is why it is possible for someone born with normal amounts of endorphin to become addicted.

One thing about alcoholism is certain: It is possible to inherit it, that is, for it to be passed from parent to child. Half of all alcoholics have an alcoholic parent, and 95 percent have a close relative who is an alcoholic. One third of all children of alcoholic parents become alcoholic. One in four marries an alcoholic. A child of an alcoholic is 5 times more likely to become an alcoholic than someone who has no family history of alcoholism. Because alcoholism seems to run in families, people with alcoholic relatives become alcoholics much faster and much more easily than other people.

Another explanation of why alcoholism seems to run in families is that it is learned behavior, that is, something you learned to do as a child. If you grow up always seeing your parent take a drink to cope with stress, to calm down, for any reason at all, you learn that that's what adults do. Then, when you become an adult, you repeat the action. Many children of alcoholics were taught by their parents that alcohol abuse was normal.

Researchers agree on one thing: You did not cause the disease. Nor did anyone else. Millions of people drink without ever becoming alcoholics. That is something you cannot teach or cause.

Getting Help

Alcoholism is *chronic*. It can never be cured. No one stops being an alcoholic. Once you have the disease, you have it for life. However, the disease can be treated. Support groups like Alcoholics Anonymous (AA) help alcoholics to stop drinking, and to stop the behavior that goes along with it. No one can make an alcoholic stop drinking except the alcoholic. He or she must really want to stop.

Alcoholics who do not drink any more are called "recovering alcoholics." They never fully recover, because the disease never goes away. However, it does not control their lives. A recovering alcoholic can never drink again, because just one drink can set the disease back in motion.

Not all alcoholics drink every day. Some drink a lot only on weekends or at parties.

Chapter 2

Warning Signs of Alcoholism

Alcoholism can take many forms. Some alcoholics only drink on the weekends. Some only drink beer. Some seem to drink all the time. There are ways of telling if your parent is an alcoholic. But each alcoholic is different. James's mother drinks during the day. She only drinks wine. Karen's father usually drinks on the weekends. But when he starts, he can't stop. Maybe your mom or dad is like Karen's or James's alcoholic parent.

If four or five of these clues are true for your parent, you have alcoholism in your family. Without help, the problem will become serious for every family member not only the one who drinks.

1) *Your parent drinks more now than he or she used to.* Karen remembers when she was younger that her father only drank late at night on the weekends. Now, he starts drinking after work on Friday and doesn't stop until Monday morning. During the week, he usually doesn't do any drinking at all.

2) *Your parent's drunken behavior is very different from his or her sober behavior.* When James's mother drinks, she is sloppy. Sometimes she slurs her words and laughs out loud to herself. She gets mad more often, and sometimes even tries to hit James. When she is sober, she seems nervous, quiet, and more helpless.

3) *Your parent denies saying or doing things that you saw when he or she was drunk.* Karen always gets in trouble when she goes out on the weekends. Even though her father gives her permission, he always yells when she gets home. He says he doesn't remember telling her she could leave. Karen cries and runs to her room.

4) *Your parent lies about how much he or she has had to drink.* When James's father gets home, he yells at his wife for drinking all day. James's mother swears that she's only had one glass of wine and complains that no one trusts her.

5) *Your parent makes excuses for needing a drink.* Whenever anyone mentions his drinking, Karen's father gets very angry. He yells about how hard he

works all week and how much his family doesn't appreciate him. He says he needs to relax on the weekends. He says he takes orders on the job, but doesn't want to be nagged in his own home.

6) *Your parent likes to drink before he or she goes out to parties.* James's mother likes to be ready an hour before she goes out for the evening. She always has three or four glasses of wine at home. She tells James that she likes to be in "the right mood" when she gets to parties.

7) *Your parent hides bottles of alcohol all over the house.* Karen finds bottles of whiskey behind the swing on the porch. Her father goes out to the porch when Karen's mom goes to bed. Sometimes

For an alcoholic whose hands shake, threading a needle can become a difficult task.

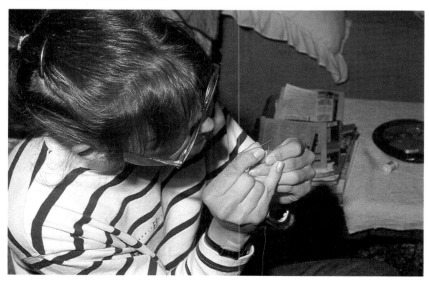

he falls asleep outside. Karen's mother cries when
she finds him there in the morning.

8) *Your parent sometimes apologizes for things he or
she did while drunk, and promises never to drink
again.* James's mother tells him how sorry she is for
missing his all-star baseball game. When James gets
home, his mother cries and promises not to drink
in the afternoon anymore.

9) *Your parent spends more and more time with
friends who also drink.* Karen and her father used to
play basketball on Saturday afternoons. These
days, Karen's father spends his weekends sitting in
the living room watching TV with his friends.
They drink all day and are very loud.

10) *Your parent's hands are not as steady as they
used to be.* James's mother used to knit and sew.
Now she says she has no patience to do work like
that. James sees his mother's hands shake when she
makes dinner and does the dishes.

11) *Your parent often drinks instead of eating
dinner.* Karen's father doesn't bother to sit down for
dinner on the weekends. Sometimes he goes out to
bars and doesn't get home until very late.

12) *Your parent doesn't keep promises.* James's
mother makes appointments to meet with James's
teachers at school, but never shows up. She
promises James that she will go, but always says
that she forgets. Each time there is a different
excuse.

Alcoholic parents may try to hide their drinking by buying alcohol secretly or hiding it around the house.

What Is Happening to Me?

Another way to test your parent's drinking problem is to look at your own behavior and feelings. See what is happening to you. Read over the following list. If four or five of these statements are true of you, there probably is an alcoholic in your house:

1) I am ashamed to bring friends home because I don't know how my alcoholic parent will behave.

2) I am sometimes afraid when my alcoholic parent is driving the car.

3) I have a hard time doing my school work because I am worried about what is happening downstairs or in the other room.

4) I sometimes think that if I were a better student, or a better athlete, or more helpful at home, my parent wouldn't drink so much.

5) When my alcoholic parent starts drinking, I am afraid someone will get hurt.

6) I sometimes want to run away from home and not have to worry about what is going to happen next.

7) I have poured out all the liquor in the house even though I knew it would get me in trouble.

8) I don't like to admit to anyone—even my best friend—that my family has this problem.

9) I don't like holidays like Thanksgiving and Christmas. In my house they always end in my parent being drunk and ruining things.

10) I sometimes think my whole family is crazy and something must be wrong with me, too.

11) I hate arguments and don't ever want to hear another one.

12) I wonder if either of my parents loves me or cares how I feel. Maybe I am just a mistake they made and can't undo now.

Chapter 3

A Family Disease

There is no such thing as the perfect family. Every family has its problems. Healthy families deal with these problems. A happy family isn't happy all the time. The difference between a happy family and an unhappy, or *dysfunctional,* family is whether the needs of all the members are met. In a healthy family, even when there's fighting and unhappiness, these basic needs are filled. But in a dysfunctional family they are not. These basic needs include survival, safety and security, love, self-esteem, and growth. In an alcoholic family some or all of these needs are neglected.

Survival is being provided with food, water, shelter, and health care. In an alcoholic home, often these simple things are not provided. A child too young to care for himself can't make food when his parent is too drunk to cook. Survival is always threatened for members of an alcoholic home.

There is no such thing as safety and security for an alcoholic family. Alcoholics are often completely unpredictable, switching from mood to mood without any warning. Alcoholic families are always on edge, wondering what the alcoholic will do next. There is no sense of security.

An alcoholic can not provide love to his family. There is saying in AA: An alcoholic is having a love affair with a bottle. To an alcoholic nothing is as important as the next drink. Not even you. That's hard to hear, but it is the nature of the disease that an alcoholic cares for nothing more than alcohol.

Members of an alcoholic family have little chance to develop self-esteem. They don't feel loved by their alcoholic parent, and so they don't feel worthy of love. Often alcoholics are verbally abusive, telling their children that they are worthless so often that the children come to believe it. A child's self-esteem has little chance in an alcoholic home.

Growth may seem to be the one thing children of alcoholics do well. They are almost always more grown-up and responsible than other people. However, this is a false growth; they are shoved into more responsibility than they can

Healthy families talk to each other. Family members take part in activities such as family dinners.

handle and skip the process of growing up. They are made by the alcoholic parent into something they are not. They don't grow on their own.

Family Roles

In a dysfunctional family, and especially in an alcoholic family, every member takes on different predictable behavior patterns. Depending on their place in the family, everyone acts a certain way.

• *The Enabler.* This usually is the alcoholic's spouse. The enabler unconsciously helps the alcoholic feed his addiction. Sometimes an enabler will protest and try to stop the alcoholic from drinking by pouring out liquor, but still cleans up after the alcoholic and lies about him to protect him. He or she will do anything to keep the uneasy peace in the family, and will try to keep the alcoholic from getting upset at all costs. The enabler thinks he or she is only trying to keep the family together, but by not allowing the alcoholic to face the consequences of his or her actions, the enabler actually helps the alcoholic to drink. Sometimes called a *co-dependent,* an enabler is actually addicted to the alcoholic in much the same way as the alcoholic is addicted to alcohol. An enabler is obsessed with the alcoholic's drinking and thinks of nothing else. It's often said that if the alcoholic has his arms wrapped around a bottle, the enabler has his arms wrapped around the alcoholic.

• *The Hero.* The hero is the perfect kid. Usually the eldest, he is an overachiever, always doing everything right. He usually takes over the responsibilities of the alcoholic. Although heroes seem to have it all together, actually they worry all the time and are easily panicked. They feel that they somehow might have caused the alcoholism by not being good enough, and so are always trying to do even better. Heroes never feel good enough, no matter how well they do.

• *The Rebel or Scapegoat.* This is often the second child in the family. As the hero slot is already filled, this child decides not to compete, but instead to get attention by being bad. He does everything wrong, always gets into trouble, is completely irresponsible. Underneath the obvious anger the rebel feels are hurt and pain. The rebel shows the bad feelings of the family, and at the same time takes attention away from the alcoholic by forcing the family to focus on his problems.

• *The Lost Child.* The lost child usually comes somewhere in the middle. When he was born, the family was too busy trying to cope with the alcoholism to give him all the attention he needed. He became withdrawn. The lost child tries to be invisible. He is terrified of anger, and in order to avoid any kind of conflict simply pretends not to exist. He is usually very lonely,

Often the spouse makes it easier for the alcoholic to go on drinking. He or she covers up the problem or hides it from the children.

and feels worthless because he gets so little attention from his family. He has never learned to relate to other people and has trouble making friends.

• *The Mascot*. This is usually the youngest child. He may seem spoilt, because he almost always gets his way. He is just so cute, the family says. He is a clown, always making jokes and jumping about. A mascot can't seem to sit still for five seconds. However, underneath the happy-go-lucky exterior of a mascot is fear. Usually a mascot has been protected from the alcoholism in the family by everyone else because he is "the baby"; he often has no idea what's going on. He knows something is wrong with the family, but the rest of the family tells him that everything is fine. He feels as if he's going crazy and becomes terrified of just about everything.

The reason everyone takes on these roles in an alcoholic home is that without these roles they would all have to deal with the pain of the alcoholism. *Denial* is very strong in an alcoholic family; no one wants to admit what's going on. Rather than talk about the alcoholism, everyone assumes these roles that allow them to function, but that also cause them pain. If an alcoholic gets help, you might think the family ought to be fine. That's not true. Everyone in the family needs help to learn to be themselves.

Chapter 4

Reaching Out for Help

You are not alone. Yours is not the only family with this terrible secret. It only seems that way. Most people don't know very much about alcoholism. Some people make fun of drunks. Others look down on them. No wonder so many alcoholics deny that anything is wrong.

You may be afraid to reach out for help. It is true that some people won't understand. But it is worth the risk. A friend or counselor can help you sort out your feelings and your choices.

A teacher, a minister, the family doctor, or a relative can give you practical help. Such a person can also give you the emotional support you need.

Look around. There must be an adult outside the family who cares about you. That person may not know very much about alcoholism. But he or she may be able to find someone who does. Or at least that person can be a good listener. It helps to talk through some of your practical decisions.

A friend your own age can like you without judging your family. You should go places and do things with friends. You need to get away from home and have some fun. You also need to spend time on your own hobbies and interests.

Support Groups And What They Can Do

Joining a support group is one of the easiest ways to get help. Many other young people have the same problem. Support groups are important in the treatment of alcoholism.

At one time in the United States alcoholism was not understood. Alcoholics were called "drunks." They were often treated badly. People thought they were weak and had no willpower. Being drunk in public was considered a crime. Doctors treated only the physical illnesses of alcoholics, such as cirrhosis of the liver.

Doctors thought that stress, such as working too hard, made people drink. They believed that if you relieved the stress, the drinking would stop. When it didn't, they said that the alcoholic wasn't trying.

That thinking was changed by two alcoholics. In 1935, a stockbroker and a doctor in Akron, Ohio, got together and helped each other stop drinking.

Drinking keeps a person from using good judgment. This is why drinking and driving is a dangerous combination.

To stay sober, they met often. They talked about their fight against their bad habit and about how it made them feel. They had a friend who worked at a local hospital. He was treating an alcoholic patient. He appealed to his friends to help out on the case.

The two men went to see the alcoholic. They helped him to stop drinking. The frank talk and support they had used with each other kept him sober too. That is how Alcoholics Anonymous was born. More than 50 years later this group still

Sometimes an alcoholic will become violent after drinking too much.

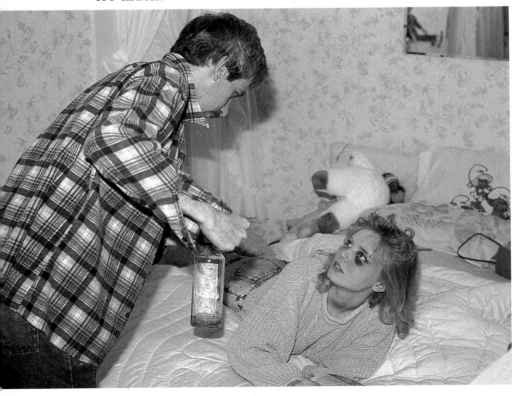

holds daily meetings. There are AA chapters in almost every community in the United States and in many foreign countries.

AA was the major source of help for alcoholics for many years. Doctors and social workers later became involved. In 1956 the medical profession finally recognized alcoholism as a disease.

Help for Families

Spouses of early members of Alcoholics Anonymous started Al-Anon. Al-Anon is a support group for the families of alcoholics. Its meetings are open to anyone who wants help.

Alateen, an AA-related group for the children of alcoholics, was founded in 1957. It was founded in California by the 17-year-old son of an alcoholic.

Most communities have an Alateen group. You can look it up in the telephone book. If there is no listing for Alateen, look for Al-Anon or Alcoholics Anonymous. Call either of those groups and ask for information about local Alateen meetings.

Alateen gatherings are very informal. They are often held in community centers or church rooms. Any young person can come. Meetings are free. Who you are doesn't matter. You don't even have to give your last name. You are welcome whether a parent is in AA or not.

Often an adult sponsor from AA gets the meeting started. But the discussion is among young

people like you who have an alcoholic parent. You
will hear some other teenagers tell their stories.
They are going through what you are going
through. Some of their experiences will be worse
than yours. Some will not be so bad.

You may feel relieved to hear other stories. You
may get some new ideas for dealing with your
problems. You will certainly get help with taking
charge of your own life.

You may be surprised to find that the talk is
very lively. There is a lot of humor in support
groups like Alateen. You may make some friends.

Alateen is not the only group for children of
alcoholics. Ask around, or look in the Yellow Pages
of your telephone book under "Alcohol Treatment
Centers."

Talk to your high school guidance counselor.
She or he may know of such a group nearby. If
there are no local programs, your guidance
counselor may be willing to start a rap session in
your school.

Your parents may be glad to have you join one
of these groups or they may not. They might think
you shouldn't talk about family problems outside.

You are not being disloyal by joining a group
that can help you. You all know that what you talk
about is private.

If your parents can't see how the group is
helping you, maybe a brother or sister will. Maybe
they, too, can reach out for help.

Chapter 5

Coping With Emergencies

Alcoholics do not use good judgment. They can do dangerous and irresponsible things. They smash up the car. They fall asleep with a cigarette in their hand and start a fire. They stumble over furniture and fall. They often take other drugs when drinking. Drugs and alcohol together can cause death. Sometimes they beat up other members of the family. Sometimes they sexually abuse their spouse or their children.

These are ugly things to think about. But many children of alcoholics have to deal with them. They are less frightening if you know *ahead of time* what to do.

Drunk Driving

Driving while drunk (what the police call "Driving While Intoxicated" or DWI) can cause trouble in the family. Alcohol slows down the thinking process and the body's responses. A drunk driver endangers passengers and everyone else on the road. Try to talk to your nonalcoholic parent about this. Your alcoholic parent should not be allowed to drive when he or she has been drinking.

You and your family must work out ways to keep your alcoholic parent out of the car when drunk. The other parent can refuse to go to a party unless it is agreed that he or she will drive home. You can certainly refuse to get in the car with a drunk driver. Learn to use buses or subways. Carry cab fare if you can afford it. Make sure you have another way to get places you need to go. Don't ride with someone who has been drinking.

Fire

Be sure you have the number of your fire department handy at all times. Work out with all the members of your family the best ways to escape from your house or apartment. Have family fire drills. Your fire department can help you plan the best ways to stay safe.

Your house should have smoke detectors. The batteries should be tested every six months or so. Put yourself in charge of this important job.

Children should talk to the nonalcoholic parent about the problem.

Medical Emergencies

Talk to your family doctor about the fastest way to get help. Alcoholics often pass out from drinking. If they have mixed alcohol with other drugs—even medicines that a doctor has given them—they may go into a coma. Someone in a coma does not respond to anything. A person in a coma can die without ever waking up. Call for help as quickly as you can.

Alcoholics often have accidents. When they are drunk they are not very good at getting help. You may have to take charge. Be sure whoever treats your parent knows that he or she has been drinking. It can make an important difference in the treatment.

As alcoholism gets worse, scary things can happen. Alcoholics can have seizures. Convulsions or seizures are sudden fits. The victim falls down and loses control of her or his body. Arms and legs jerk wildly for several minutes. Then the person falls into a deep sleep. You should call a doctor. Loosen your parent's collar. Remove objects that he or she might hit and be hurt by. There isn't much else you can do.

Delirium tremens (DT's) can strike an advanced alcoholic. Someone with DT's shakes a lot and can't stop. This is as scary to the alcoholic as to others who see him or her. An alcoholic with DT's can have *hallucinations*. These are visions that are only in the person's mind. But they are very real to him or her. And they are often very scary. Call for medical help right away. There is nothing else you can do.

Physical Violence and Sexual Abuse

There may not be a way to stop an alcoholic from verbally abusing others. But we have laws to protect people from physical abuse. There are trained experts in every community who are ready to help.

If you are abused by an alcoholic parent, you can get help. Talk to an adult friend—a minister or rabbi, a teacher, a counselor, a doctor, a trusted relative. Ask where to go for help in your community. Or you can look in the telephone book. Check under "Child Abuse" in the white pages or "Human Services" in the Yellow Pages.

You may find only a drug abuse or alcohol abuse "hotline" number. These lines are answered by people trained to help in emergencies. The person who picks up your call may be able to tell you where to call or go for help.

If your alcoholic parent beats you, or your other parent, or a sister or brother, you can call the police. Go to a neighbor's house to use the telephone. Both your parents may be angry with you for doing this. They may feel that outside people should not be involved. They may think you have given away the family secret. You must use your judgment. Is the situation bad enough to risk their anger? Will they both seek help if they see how serious things are?

Get help if you are afraid that your alcoholic parent will hurt someone in the family. Talk with a trusted adult friend or relative about your fears. Don't wait until it happens again if you are scared. If your alcoholic parent hits you often, you need help. If your alcoholic parent tries to abuse you or a brother or sister, that is a good reason to ask for help.

Getting help is sometimes not easy. Ask an adult you trust to go with you. If the abuse is severe, you may be taken out of your home. That is a drastic step. But if things are very bad, it may be the only way to make them better.

No one deserves abuse. No one should be abused with words or with fists. No one should have to suffer sexual abuse. Every child deserves loving parents. If your family life is difficult, you will have to learn to accept it. What you *can* do is to make your *own* life different.

You can choose to take responsibility for yourself and your life. You can decide to help yourself. And you don't have to do it alone. Many support groups and social service agencies are willing to help you. You *can* take control of your own life. We will talk more about this in Chapter 8, "Looking at the Future."

Chapter 6

What You Can Do For Yourself

Alcoholic parents love their children as much as other parents do. That may be hard for you to believe. Your alcoholic parent may have said and done some terrible things to you in drunken rages.

Joanne's mother said that having a child like Joanne made her drink.

George's father told him that he was a stupid embarrassment to the family. He locked George out of the house for 24 hours.

Gracie's father told her she was a slut because she went to the movies with a boy in her class.

Louise's father accused her of forgetting to iron his shirts. Then he beat her for it.

41

What or Who Is at Fault?

How can these be actions of loving parents? The actions are not loving. They are cruel. But they are the actions of people with minds crazed by alcohol. The drug made these parents do what they did. The disease is more at fault than the parent.

Does that mean you should stand for such abuse? Absolutely not. Your parent should not be allowed to mistreat you.

If you are abused, you have a right to be angry. You should be angry. But try to focus your anger on the action and on the disease. Try not to be angry at your alcoholic parent. It is the drunkenness and the behavior that you hate, not your parent. It is hard to separate the two when you are being abused. Think about it later. It will help.

You may still have good moments with your alcoholic parent. If you do, you should cherish them. But that doesn't mean that you should put up with your parent's drunken behavior.

What You Can Do

You can gain more control over your own life. Separate your feelings about your parent from your feelings about the disease and what it makes your parent do. This process is called *detachment*.

A support group can help the family of an alcoholic to work out its
problems.

You cannot make your parent stop drinking. That is a hard fact, but you must face it. Maybe you have tried. Maybe you have thrown out all the bottles in the liquor cabinet. Maybe you have even convinced your parent to promise to stop. You may be holding your breath, hoping it will work this time.

Your parent wants to keep the promise. Your parent probably loves you very much. But alcoholics lose control over their actions. They can't help it.

You can't make your parent stop drinking. That is a losing battle. But you *can* keep your parent from hurting you anymore. That is a fight worth putting your energy into.

You can help your alcoholic parent most by helping yourself. You can become a healthy person with a full, rich life. No parent could want more for a child.

Taking Control

How do you take control of your own life? First you separate your feelings about your parent from your feelings about what alcohol makes your parent do. Then begin to express your feelings.

If you love your parent, say so. You may hate things your parent does or says when drunk. If you do, say so when he or she is sober and able to listen. Talk to your nonalcoholic parent about all your feelings.

Break the rule of silence in your family. Having an alcoholic in the family can cause many problems. Look for quiet times to talk about the problems. Then talk about practical solutions.

You know, for example, that arguing with a drunk parent won't do any good. She or he won't remember it in the morning. You will be tired out and hurt. You will be frustrated. So don't do it.

When your drunk parent tries to start a fight, walk away from it. Take a stroll around the block if you can get away. Or walk into another room. Detach yourself emotionally from hurtful things your alcoholic parent says to you. He or she probably doesn't mean them.

Tell yourself, "That is the alcohol talking, and I don't need to hear it." If your parent insults you, remind yourself that the insult isn't true.

Don't let your alcoholic parent draw you into a fight with your other parent. You can say, "I love you both, but this is not my fight. You will have to settle it between yourselves."

Practical Solutions

Jerry couldn't study for exams. His parents' fighting kept him from doing his school work at home. He asked for permission to work at the library. He promised to be home by 9:30 each night. His parents were surprised at his request, but they agreed.

Marianne's mother got drunk every afternoon. Marianne went home after school to baby-sit with a four-year-old brother and a three-year-old sister. She wanted to go out for basketball, but she couldn't go for practice in the afternoon. She was worried about what would happen to the younger children. She finally got up the courage to talk with her father. He hired a part-time housekeeper so that Marianne could go to practice. She was glad the family could afford to pay for help.

Michelle wasn't as lucky. She was scared of driving home from night band practice with her alcoholic father. She asked her mother to drive her home. Michelle's mother refused. She didn't see her husband's driving as a serious problem. She told Michelle that her fears were silly. Michelle tried to work something out. No one else in the band lived near her, so she couldn't ask other parents for a ride. Her mother said taking a bus at that hour was not safe. So Michelle gave up band. The price was high, but she chose not to drive with a drunk.

Taking control of your life often calls for hard choices. You know that you must be responsible for your own life. You know that there are things in your life that you can't change. But you don't always know what to do.

It helps to have somebody outside the family to talk to about all these things.

Chapter 7

What You Can Do For the Alcoholic

Alcoholism counselors found out something very important. By treating the whole family, they can often help bring the alcoholic person into treatment before he or she hits bottom.

Why must they treat the whole family? People in the family become codependents or enablers. They help the alcoholic drink by covering up for him or her. A wife calls the alcoholic's office for him. She says her husband has the flu when he really has a hangover. She is helping him drink. The wife should refuse to call his office. The husband should have to face the results of his drinking himself.

**...many alcoholics will go into
treatment if their job is threatened.**

A daughter sweeps up all the glassware that her
alcoholic mother threw at her father. She is
protecting her mother's dependency on alcohol.
That mother should have to clean up the broken
glass herself. She needs to see the mess she made
while she was drinking.

Even a boss can be an enabler. She or he likes
the alcoholic. He is a nice guy. So the boss accepts
weak excuses for missed days on the job. After a
while the boss doesn't expect as much of the
alcoholic. So the alcoholic doesn't see that his
drinking is a threat. He doesn't realize that he can
lose his job because of his drinking.

That's too bad, because many alcoholics will go
into treatment if their job is threatened. When they
are made to see how their drinking hurts them and
their families, many alcoholics will go for help.

What Alcoholism Counselors Can Do

Alcoholism counselors have found a way to help
families, close friends, and people at work.
Counselors teach them to show alcoholics how
much pain their drinking has caused. The process
is called *intervention*. People who care step in and

Cleaning up after the alcoholic is often an attempt to hide the problem.

try to help. It often gets the alcoholic to enter a treatment program.

You can't do this by yourself. It takes skill and experience. But you can talk to your family about getting help. You can suggest an alcoholism counseling service.

A counseling service could help each member of the family to change. You can all learn to stop helping the alcoholic to drink. Counseling can also help each of you to take charge of your own life.

Treatment for the Alcoholic

If you can get the alcoholic to go to a treatment center, that is a good first step. It is the beginning of a long road back for the whole family.

The alcoholic must first dry out in a hospital or clinic. Doctors need to treat withdrawal symptoms. Those are the body's reaction to not getting alcohol. Some are very serious. It is hard for the body to get back to normal.

When the body is free of alcohol, an alcoholic must begin counseling. Learning to live without alcohol is called *rehabilitation*. Many treatment centers have AA groups that meet right there. The hospital stay is about 28 days. Then the recovering alcoholic is ready to go home. She or he will be encouraged to join AA or another alcoholism

Getting an alcoholic to a treatment center is a good first step.

group. Joining a support group helps recovering alcoholics to stay sober. They can live a normal life as long as they never have another drink.

A recovering alcoholic must work to stay sober, day by day. He or she can never drink again. It will help if the family stays in counseling for a while. The family can gain strength together. Family members can learn healthy ways to get along. Each member can learn how to take charge of his or her own life.

Helping Yourself

Maybe you and your family can get your alcoholic parent into treatment. Maybe you can't. Counseling can help you and your family even if the alcoholic refuses treatment.

As hard as it may be, you must focus on your own life. You may love your parent very much. But you must think about yourself. Stop helping your alcoholic parent drink. Start helping yourself to live.

Family members can learn healthy ways to get along. Each member can learn how to take charge of his or her own life.

Chapter 8

Looking at the Future

Everything you've learned in this book will help you to create your own life. That means separating yourself from your parent's disease. It also means taking control of your life.

You can succeed in whatever you do. One way to do that is to try to find the positive side of your experiences. Ask yourself what you have learned from the experience.

In living with an alcoholic parent, you may have learned many things. It may have been important for you to work on your self-esteem every day, for example. Or you may have learned that you were able to make tough decisions. You may have learned to be more independent and self-reliant than other kids. You learned about the dangers of alcohol abuse first-hand. You know how alcoholism can destroy a family.

Improving your own life doesn't mean you must forget your family. It means you must do all you can to understand them. By remembering your alcoholic parent's struggle with their disease, you may make better decisions about your own life. Get involved with support groups that will help you to understand fully how the disease of alcoholism works, and how each family member is affected.

Good counseling can help you to see things more clearly. It can teach you what your special needs are. It is a chance to talk about the kinds of relationships that will be healthy for you in the future.

Alcoholism does seem to run in families. You need to be aware of how dangerous it may be for you to drink, even a little. But be careful of making excuses for your behavior. There may be times when it seems easier to blame your family background for your own poor choices. You don't want to make the same mistakes that your alcoholic parent made.

Children of alcoholic parents may have to work harder to restore or maintain a positive self-image. But they can recover. They can take responsibility for their actions. They can set their own goals and work toward reaching them.

If you are a child of an alcoholic parent, take time to concentrate on yourself. You are a valuable person. When you build yourself a happy life, you will be able to share it with others.

It is important for children of an alcoholic to pursue their own interests.

Facts and Figures

The problem of alcoholism is real and is a major problem in the United States. If you have an alcoholic relative, you are far from alone.

• There are about 11 million alcoholics in the US., including 3.3 million 12 to 17-year-olds.

• 7 million kids under age 20 live with an alcoholic.

• Alcohol is involved in 64 percent of all murders.

• Alcohol is involved in 33 percent of all suicides.

• Alcohol is involved in 50 percent of all fatal falls.

• Alcohol is involved in 68 percent of all deaths by drowning.

• Alcohol is involved in 80 percent of all fires.

- Alcohol is involved in 55 percent of all arrests.

- Alcohol is involved in 60 percent of child abuse.

- Alcohol is involved in 50 percent of all traffic deaths.

- Alcoholism is the third highest cause of death, killing 205, 000 people a year.

- Alcoholism costs US businesses about $43 billion a year.

- One in four families is affected by alcoholism.

- Alcoholics are 11 times more likely to get divorced.

- Alcoholic families pay twice the amount of health care of other families.

- About 41 percent of the adult population has suffered some kind of harm from someone else's drinking problem.

Glossary—*Explaining New Words*

addict A person who is dependent on a drug and cannot control his or her use of it.

alcoholic A person who is addicted to alcohol. Someone who cannot stop drinking once he or she has started, whether it is every day or once every six months.

chemical dependence Need for a drug (alcohol or any other addictive substance) in order to get along without withdrawal symptoms.

co-dependent A person whose actions help a dependent continue his or her addiction.

dependent A person who is chemically dependent or psychologically dependent on a drug.

depression Feeling very low for a long period of time.

DTs (*delirium tremens*) Uncontrollable shaking brought on by drinking too much alcohol for too long a period of time.

dysfunctional (*family*) A family that functions in unhealthy ways.

enabler Like a co-dependent, a person who assists the addict in his or her dependency on a drug.

hallucinations Visions, sometimes terrible, of people and events seen in the mind. They seem very real to the person having them.

hereditary Passed from parents to children. Hair color and eye color are examples of physical hereditary factors.

intervention A process that helps alcoholics face the results of their addiction. Family, friends, and people from work are involved in bringing alcoholics to treatment.

psychological dependence Need for a drug to deal with stress or stressful emotions.

role model Someone who serves as an example for others.

social drinker A person who can enjoy alcoholic drinks on social occasions without becoming addicted.

stress Mental or emotional pressure.

withdrawal symptoms Upsetting physical and mental effects that alcoholics and other addicts suffer when they give up the drug that they are physically dependent on.

Where to Go for Help

The quickest source of information and help on alcoholism is your telephone book. You can find listings under "Alcoholism Information and Treatment Centers" in the Yellow Pages or under "Alcohol . . ." in the white pages. Also, try your public library for reading material. Look up "Alcoholism" in the subject file, or ask a librarian to help you.

If your community search doesn't satisfy you, you can write to any of these organizations for more information:

Alcoholics Anonymous (AA)
General Service Office
P.O. Box 459
Grand Central Station
New York, NY 10163

AA publishes literature on alcoholism. National AA can refer you to meetings in your community.

Al-Anon/Alateen Family
 Groups
P.O. Box 182
Madison Square Station
New York, NY 10159
 This is the central
clearing house for
information on Alateen
groups and Adult
Children of Alcoholics
groups. They also
publish pamphlets and
books on living with an
alcoholic.

Children of Alcoholics
 Foundation
540 Madison Avenue
New York, NY 10022
 Publishes research
reports on children of
alcoholics. It also keeps a
file of community
resources.

Community Intervention
220 South 10th Street
Minneapolis, MN 55403
 A resource for adults
who want to start support
groups for teen children
of alcoholics.

National Association for
Children of Alcoholics
13706 Coast Highway
South Laguna, CA 92677
 A national advocacy
group for children of
alcoholics. It also
prepares some
publications.

National Clearinghouse
for Alcohol Information
P.O. Box 2345
Rockville, MD 20852
 Bibliographies and
publications are either
free or available for a
small fee.

For Further Reading

Brooks, Cathleen. *The Secret Everyone Knows*. San Diego, CA: Operation Cork, 1981, 40 pages. An overview of the problem of living with alcoholic parents.

Leite, Evelyn and Pamela Espeland. *Different Like Me: A Book for Teens Who Worry About Their Parents' Use of Alcohol and Drugs*. Minneapolis, MN: Johnson Institute Books, 1987, 110 pages. Shared experiences of young people who have alcoholic parents plus some positive ideas and rules for coping.

Maxwell, Ruth. *Beyond the Booze Bottle: What to Do When Alcohol or Chemical Dependency Hits Close to Home*. New York: Ballantine, 1986, 290 pages. The founder of a new family treatment program follows the case histories of three families.

McFarland, Rhoda. *Drugs and Your Parents*, rev. ed. New York: The Rosen Publishing Group, Inc., 1993, 64 pages. This book helps the younger reader to understand chemical dependency. It explains the effects on the family as well as the addicted person.

Scales, Cynthia G. *Potato Chips for Breakfast*. Stroudsburg, PA: Quotidian, 1986, 160 pages. The autobiography of an alcoholic treatment counselor who grew up in an alcoholic home and comes to understand her patients through her own experience.

Seixas, Judith S. *Living with a Parent Who Drinks Too Much*. New York: Greenwillow, 1979, 128 pages. An alcoholism counselor talks about the effects of the disease on young people.

Index

About the Author
Nancy Shuker is a free-lance writer and editor based in New York. A former editor at Time-Life Books and executive editor of several consumer and business newsletters, she is also an adult child of an alcoholic parent.

About the Editor
Evan Stark is a well-known sociologist, educator, and therapist as well as a popular lecturer on women's and children's health issues. Dr. Stark was the Henry Rutgers Fellow at Rutgers University, an associate at the Institute for Social and Policy Studies at Yale University, and a Fulbright Fellow at the University of Essex. He is the author of many publications in the field of family relations and is the father of four children.

Photo Credits
Photos by Stuart Rabinowitz